Creating Love And Respect In Families: From Generation To Generation

Linda G. Bell, Ph.D.

Dedication: To Claire, Eric, Michael and Jessica

Preface

This book summarizes a three generational study of love and respect in families in the U.S. and Japan. Like many people who are drawn to family studies, my initial motivation was rooted in my own family experience. My father grew up in poverty; my mother in a working class family. I was much loved in my family, but I didn't exactly fit in. I always experienced myself as special, and an unspoken anxiety engulfed me and my mother. There was always the understanding in my mind that I was not to get my father angry; his anger would be dangerous. I was mystified. My father would sometimes shout, but he never hit.

There was another very important person involved in the family dynamic; he was my biological father, and this was the big family secret. I didn't figure it out until I was in college. This man played a major role in our family. He and my dad were friends. He set my dad up in business running a pool hall. He gave me presents: books, clothes, a saxophone.

When I told my mother that I knew about my biological father, she told me that she had feared for our lives, thinking that my dad might kill us if he knew. I was born in the 1940s. I suspect that my dad knew from the get-go but loved me anyway. Everyone went along with the pretend.

Growing up I wanted to be a psychologist in order to help people; unconsciously, I think, I wanted to help myself and understand my family. During my psychology internship I learned about a new treatment approach called family therapy. I became very excited about family therapy and decided to enter a 2-year training program to learn how to do it. I also planned my research around studying families. I wanted to demonstrate how family dynamics affected children. I was particularly interested in work being done in the area of validation or acknowledgement. Acknowledgement allows the other person, in this case children growing up in the family, to have their own ideas and feeling – not being told what their feelings are or what they must believe. A non-validating response to an angry child might be "You're not angry; you're just tired. Go to bed." Or "You don't hate your sister; we love each other in this family." A non-validating family belief might be that all family members should hold the same ideas and feelings. "If you disagree with me, it means that you don't love me."

Looking back now, after years of teaching and learning about family dynamics and family therapy – and also years of dealing with my own anxiety – I think that deep down I wanted to know if and how people could be both loved and respected. I always felt I was loved by both of my parents, but something else was not right; I couldn't really be myself. My research, then, ended up focusing on two major processes: affection and respect. Respect for each individual's ideas and feelings. I found out that it's possible to love people you don't respect – and to respect people you don't love. Basically, I was loved but not validated or acknowledged for who I was. I had to be someone else in order to survive in my family.

This book is about my 40-year journey to learn about more and less healthy families, and how those families affect the development of children. The research is about affection and respect in families, about how family patterns are reflected in the lives of family members, particularly children, and about how family influence persists through time – even through the generations.

My primary research colleague was David Bell, my husband, who is a sociologist. There were many others who helped

Linda Bell

with the research. I am grateful to all of the individuals and families who participated in the various telephone and home interviews, and grateful to all of the students and research assistants who interviewed families and individuals, and to those who coded interviews. This research took me into the homes of many families -- both in the U.S. and in Japan. I'll take you along on my journey. Hopefully it will be enjoyable and educational.

Acknowledgements

247 families in the U.S. and Japan participated in family interviews in their homes. To these folks I am very grateful. Over a hundred colleagues, research assistants, and students helped with designing the study and the instruments, interviewing families in their homes and by phone, and coding taped marital and family discussions. Obviously, without this support over the 40 years of the project, the research would not have been possible. Particular thanks go to Lena Ericksen, Connie Cornwell, Yojiro Nakata, Hisako Dendo, Tsunetsugu Munakata, and to my primary co-investigator, David C. Bell. Original funding for the project was from the National Institute of Mental Health. Additional support followed from The Family Institute at Northwestern University, the University of Houston – Clear Lake, the Texas State Coordinating Board for Higher Education, and Indiana University Purdue University Indianapolis.

Linda Bell

To grow mature is to separate more distinctly, to connect more closely.

HUGO VON HOFMANNSTHAL, THE BOOK OF FRIENDS, 1922

CONTENTS

Linda Bell

Chapter 1
Normal Families

I was introduced to family therapy and to family theory during my psychology internship. I was immediately engaged with this new way of thinking about human problems and later pursued a two-year training program in family therapy at The Family Institute, currently affiliated with Northwestern University. I read the available research on how families influenced the health of individual family members. This research tended to focus on clinical situations. Particularly on how family communication patterns influenced the mental health of children growing up in the family. There was talk of the schizophrenogenic mother, for instance, suggesting that mothers who put their children in double binds (damned if you do damned if you don't situations) could cause them to become schizophrenic. We are way past that now, but for a time it was a common way of thinking.

I decided that I wanted to study "normal" families, not families of mentally ill individuals. I wanted to study families of adolescents, as adolescence is a critical time for the development of independent thinking. I also wanted a homogeneous sample for statistical reasons. I felt that if I tried to cover too much territory (too many different kinds of families) in one study, it would doom the statistics. There would be too much variation for me to see any clear pattern in the family's influence on the individual. Since I was female, I decided to study girls. I wanted families where the girl was the oldest child (like me), but I couldn't find a large enough sample that way. I also wanted 2-child families because it would make tape-recording easier – but again, in order to recruit a large enough sample, I had to include families with 2 or 3 children, one of whom was a 16 or 17-year-old daughter. I recruited families through high schools. The sample turned out to be white middle class because of the school superintendent who agreed to allow me access to his school district, a district made up of white middle class families.

The Families

In the mid 1970s, a research assistant and I gathered data on 99 U.S. families during home interviews. The families were recruited through three high schools in a suburban school district. The families had two parents and two or three children; at least one of whom was an adolescent daughter. Almost all of the parents grew up during the Depression and married after World War II. About a fourth of these mothers and fathers had at least one parent who was an immigrant from Europe, mostly from northern or eastern Europe. The results reported in this book are for the parents who grew up during the Depression, their children and their grandchildren. Findings might vary if we looked at a different historical period, a different ethnic group, or a different socioeconomic group.

In the mid 1980s I went to Japan with my family on a 2-year sabbatical. With the collaboration of Japanese colleagues, home interviews were completed with 62 Japanese families. The Japanese families were middle class, had two parents and two to four children, including at least one adolescent.

Study Overview

All families, in the U.S. and in Japan, participated in a

home interview in which each family member completed a true/false questionnaire describing their family. Couples, and later the family as a whole, then discussed items on which they had disagreed, and tried to reach agreement. This is called a "revealed difference" exercise because the family would read one item at a time, noting which member(s) said true and which said false. Then they would discuss each item, attempt to reach agreement on the correct answer, and then note whether the answer was true or false, or that they had no agreement.

The family then completed a family picture together. The family was given colored circles for people, red and black lines of different lengths to stretch between them to show similarity or difference, and loops made of yarn to show individual boundaries, coalitions, and larger groups. All of the activities were taped. Later, research team members coded the tapes for various family measures – like mood, problem-solving ability, respect, caring, and conflict.

Some twenty-five years after the home interviews, family members (both elder parents and the midlife adult former adolescents, both daughters and sons) participated in telephone interviews focusing on wellbeing and on the relationships between the adult children and their elder parents. For the U.S. sample, home interviews then followed with 44 elder couples, and also with 88 then adult children who had families with adolescents of their own. For the adult children's families, the original interview was repeated in order for us to compare families across the generations

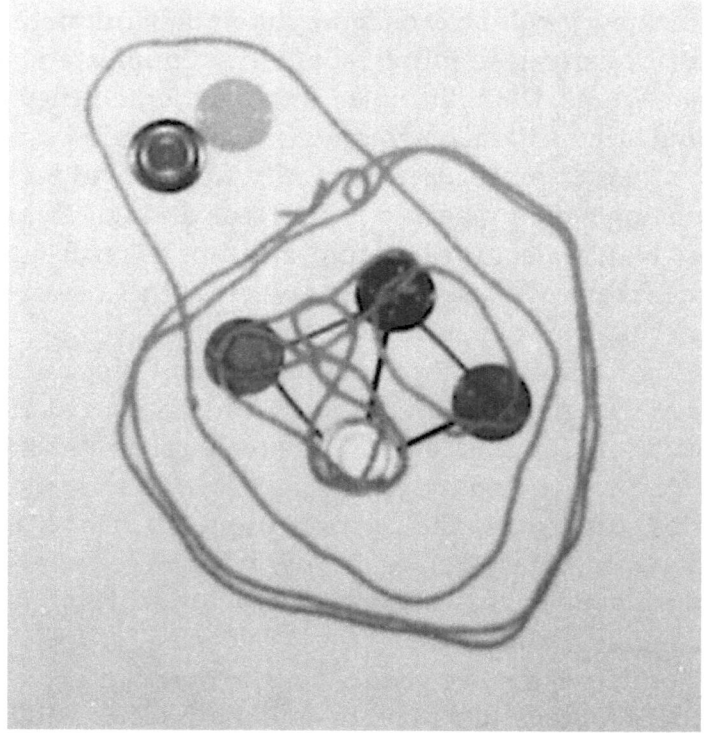

Grandparents (U.S. picture). This family has two family boundaries, one that includes the parents and kids, and one that includes them and the grandparents. The one that includes only the immediate family is stronger (double boundary).

Chapter 2
Family Process

Attachment theory, developed by John Bowlby (1907 – 1990), is a major relationship theory today. Attachment and caregiving are two aspects of any close relationship. Historically the emphasis has been on the caregiver-infant relationships, particularly the child's attachment paired with the mother's caregiving. In the 1930s Bowlby studied delinquent boys, and in the 1940s, children separated from their families by war. He focused on the child's fear of abandonment and loss. Bowlby introduced the concept of attachment to help explain the anxiety that very young children exhibit upon separation from their parents or parental figures and the signs of joy they exhibit upon reunion. He rejected the Freudian assertion that caregiving centers on a baby's need for food or shelter, proposing instead that caregiving is associated with the infant's need for emotional support and protection from predators. Whereas Freud conceptualized the child as responding primarily to physical care such as feeding, Bowlby asserted that the fundamental bond is based on comfort and physical contact.

Bowlby's ideas received support from the work of two other researchers, Harry Harlow and Renee Spitz. Harry Harlow was a psychologist who showed that infant monkeys preferred soft cloth pretend mothers – rather than wire pretend mothers who provided milk. Renee Spitz studied babies in hospitals and saw that those who were never touched did not thrive - sometimes, did not even survive. When nurses in the United States saw films that Spitz had made, they moved to open children's wards in hospitals to parents. Before then, it had been thought better to keep the children separated to avoid germs. When my husband was hospitalized as a child, his mother was allowed in one hour each day with him. She could tell he was doing poorly when the toy she left one day was exactly where she had left it the next day.

A child who is securely attached to its mother – or another primary caregiver -- will explore freely while the mother is present, will engage with strangers, may be visibly upset when the mother departs, and happy to see the mother return. As an adult, a person with a history of secure attachment will be able to form lasting, mutually caring relationships with others. A person who enjoyed a much less secure relationship as a child may be anxious in relationships and concerned with abandonment as an adult. They may tend to avoid making relationships at all since relationships have been previously experienced as unsafe and uncaring.

Attachment researchers talk about a caregiver as providing both a *safe haven* and a *secure base* to the developing child. The caregiver is a safe haven when he or she provides emotional support, protection and comfort. As a child matures, the caregiver provides a secure base from which the child can venture into the larger world, a safe place to return to after exploring a sometimes scary world. I remember how surprised I was at how often my toddler would turn to look at me while being engaged in play. When a child feels insecure or concerned by what is going on, they can return to their secure base to recoup.

In our work we use the term connection to refer to a relationship where attachment is matched with caregiving. A relationship is high in connection when caregiving creates secure attachment. A relationship is low in connection when inconsistent or inadequate caregiving creates insecure attachment. This pattern mostly reflects the safe haven aspect in Bowlby's theory.

As the child explores the world in the context of a secure base, the child comes to see themselves as effective and in control. We call this process individuation. The child in a highly individuated relationship is characterized by feeling competent, and by knowing who they are. A child with an insecure base finds exploring the world produces uncertainty and anxiety. This child is characterized by less certainty about who they are and what they can do. Adult relationships can also provide safe havens that provide connection and secure bases that foster individuation.

Our research has focused on these two concepts: connection and individuation. The connection process involves attachment and affection. Dependency is met with nurture, resulting in a warm, accepting family climate that encourages self-esteem and ability to trust. The individuation process involves validation and respect. Expression of feelings and thoughts is met with acknowledgement, resulting in a family where family members see each other as unique individuals, each with their own particular ideas and feelings. For children this supports the development of a strong sense of self as an individual, a personal identity, and nurtures autonomy. Connection and individuation are independent processes; that is, you can imagine a family that is high on both, low on both, high on one and low on the other, or somewhere in the middle.

Connection Process

So how does this work in a family? A family scoring high on connection has a climate that's warm and accepting. This allows individuals to trust enough to depend on others and ask for what they need. Asking and depending results in receiving support and nurture from others. Children then can develop a positive self-esteem because they feel they are cherished by others.

In a negative process neglect, or possibly abuse, creates a cold, rejecting family climate. This kind of atmosphere inhibits the development of both self-esteem and the ability to trust. It reduces the likelihood of a child depending on parents to meet

14

their needs, leading instead to self-protection, defensiveness, and an unwillingness to become vulnerable by exposing needs and desires. A child who feels safe can cry or ask for hugs. A child who is fearful may keep quiet and try not to draw attention.

Families scoring high on measures of connection are described by coders as having a warm and supportive mood during their discussions of differences during the revealed difference exercise. They exhibit joking and humor and have little overt conflict. Families scoring low on connection are often described as have a sad or depressed mood and as having more overt conflict, more arguing or fighting amongst themselves.

To increase connection in your family, listen carefully when your children talk to you. Make eye contact. Take time, be calm, smile, nod your head. Touch people to let them know you care, and that you are paying attention to them. Holding and hugs are great ways to nurture your mate, your children, others in your family. Find a way to stop what you're doing and take time to pay attention when your child or mate is sad and needs support. Plan family time, or family activities, when you can just be together and enjoy each other's company.

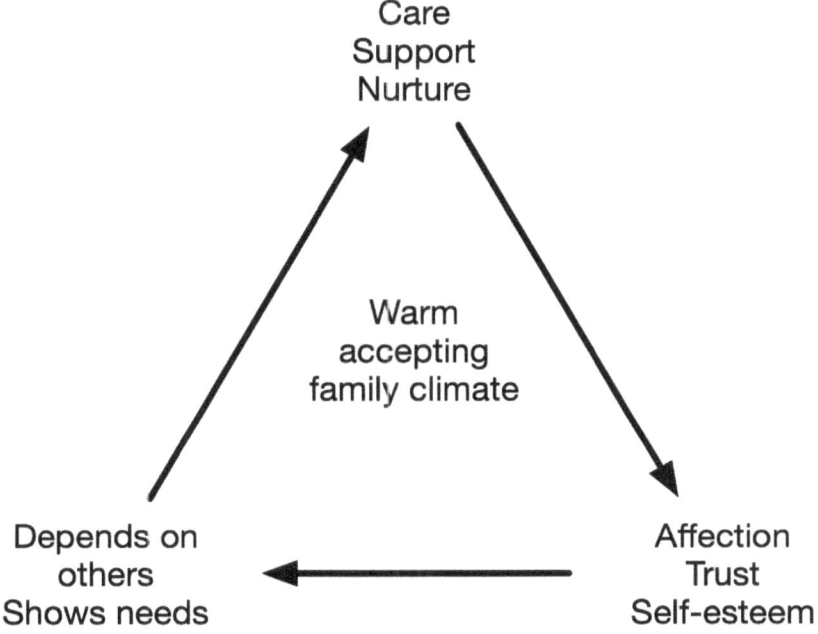

Connection Process (love, affection, trust). A warm, accepting family climate supports adults and children to be open about their vulnerabilities and needs. People can depend on each other for care, support, and nurture. Thus, individuals develop affection for themselves and others. This process nurtures self-esteem and the ability to trust others.

Individuation process

In a highly individuated family, the individuals in the family feel respected. They listen to and acknowledge the contributions of others and validate those contributions. The unspoken family rule is that it's OK to be different from others; it's OK to disagree. Disagreement doesn't threaten the security of the family. As ideas are valued and validated, family members develop a positive sense of who they are as distinguished from

others. When children's ideas and feelings are sought and acknowledged, it strengthens their sense of a personal identity; it gives
them confidence in their own ideas and thus the ability to behave
with autonomy. In a negative process, discomfort with individual differences can lead to invalidation or mystification ("You're
not angry, you're tired."). There is pressure to be the same as other
family members, for all family members to have the same needs,
values and wants. It is difficult for a child to form a clear sense of
their individuality or behave with autonomy.

Families scoring high on measures of individuation are
described as being comfortable discussing differences and disagreements. People take responsibility for their own actions,
feeling and thoughts, and do not take responsibility for the actions, feelings or thoughts of others. In other words, each person
has a personal identity; individuality is respected. Thus, family members are good at discussing disagreements and resolving them. Families low on individuation may be overly close or
overly concerned with each other. Their desire for everyone to
think the same is challenged by the revealed difference exercise.
Family members often appear to have hidden conflict which they
don't discuss because disagreement is uncomfortable or scary.

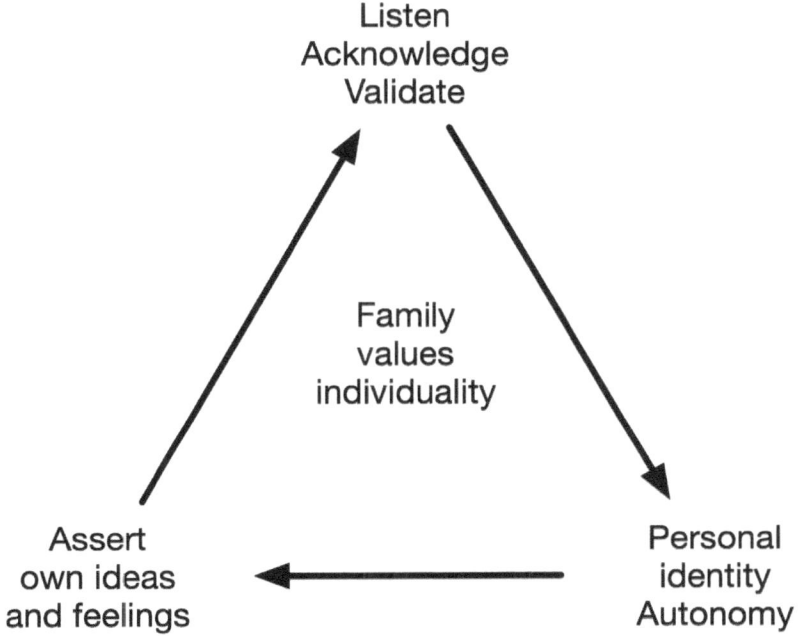

Listen
Acknowledge
Validate

Family
values
individuality

Assert
own ideas
and feelings

Personal
identity
Autonomy

Individuation Process (respect, validation, individuality). Family members value individuality and respect individual differences. Thus, adults and children are free to assert themselves and express personal ideas and feelings. People listen to each other; they acknowledge and validate each other. This process nurtures a sense of personal identity and personal autonomy.

To increase individuation in your family, remember that each person is unique – and special. Nurture each child's ability to express their ideas and feelings; listen to them with an open heart. Ask for each person's input in a discussion; let them know you want to know what they think and feel. Don't belittle them for what they think or feel. It's OK to disagree, to express another point of view. Cherish each person for who they are, as special, unique people. Even when we disagree, we're both OK. We can't be expected to agree on everything because we are different people.

We used several scales to evaluate connection and individuation when coding the family discussions. Examples from the scales follow. The first four are associated with connection; the second four with individuation. (-) means this was a negative measure of the concept:

WARMTH AND SUPPORT:

The family has an atmosphere of openness, comfortableness, optimism & warmth.

The family's mood is Very Cold ...to...Very Warm.

DEPRESSION (-):

The family has an atmosphere of depression, sadness, hopelessness.

Family's mood is Very Cheerful...to...Very Sad.

HUMOR:

Family's use of joking and humor (none or almost none...to...very often).

Amount of laughter (none or almost none...to...very often).

OVERT CONFLICT (-):

Overt conflict in the family is severe (little or none...to... impairs group functioning).

RESPECT FOR INDIVIDUALITY:

In general family members take responsibility for their own actions, feeling, and thoughts, and do not take responsibility for the actions, feelings or thoughts of others.

COMFORT WITH DIFFERENCES AND DISAGREEMENT:

Family members seem comfortable with differences or disagreements.

Family members do not avoid differences and disagreements.

COVERT CONFLICT (conflict that is hidden, covered up) (-)

Covert conflict in the family is severe (little or none...to... impairs group functioning).

How were feelings expressed? (very directly or openly...to...very indirectly or covertly).

PROBLEM-SOLVING EFFICIENCY:

Family's efficiency at problem solving was Very Inefficient...to...Very Efficient.

Connection and individuation often go together. Well-functioning young people report a close connection with parents while at the same time demonstrating high levels of autonomy and individuality. Healthy parent-child connection can support healthy individuation. One of the earlier family therapists, Carl Whitaker, suggested that family members can only be as connected as they are separate; that a family's capacity to be intimate and caring and their capacity to be separate and independent develop together. People can't risk being close unless they have the ability to be separate—it's too frightening to be deeply involved if you aren't sure you can be separate and stand on your own. Individuals also can't risk being truly independent or separate when they don't have a safe, warm and caring base to return to.

Thus, connection and individuation can support one another. I often think of couples as two pendulums, the closer they swing together, the further they can swing apart. Independence and autonomy make it safer for me to get close to others without fear of "losing myself." And a close secure relationship gives me courage to act independently in other aspects of my life. Often, the more independent we become, the easier it is to risk being intimate and close. The more secure we feel with intimacy and closeness, the easier it is to act independently.

Chapter 3
Boundaries Around
And Within Families

Most families have some kind of boundary – a sense of who's in the family and who's not in the family. This boundary is closed or open to various degrees. Larry Constantine described different kinds of family boundaries in his book, *Family Paradigms*.

In a family with a tightly closed boundary, the boundary around the family is strong and keeps most people out. Constantine calls this a **closed** family. The outside world is perceived as unhealthy or dangerous. Family members feel that children left without strong guidance are not safe. The family provides security and protection. Individuals generally have a strong sense of loyalty to the family. Often in a family with a tightly closed boundary, individuality is weak. Disagreement, difference and anger are negatives. Family members agree with each other about values and about the rules concerning how to behave. The motto for this family could be "Stability though tradition and loyalty."

Another pattern is the family with a very open boundary. Constantine calls this a **random** family. Friends and visitors move easily in and out of the family. Innovation and change are comfortable. Personal freedom and individuality are highly valued. The alternative to individual freedom is experienced as oppression. In this family the expression of feelings is more spontaneous, often passionate. There tends to be a high tolerance for differences and ambiguity. The family nurtures and validates creativity in its members. A motto might be "Variety through innovation and individuality."

Many families fall somewhere between closed and random. Constantine calls this an **open** family. The family seeks stability and security while also valuing individuality and creativity. Differences and disagreement can be discussed and there is a focus on problem solving, on reaching a decision everyone can live with. A motto might be "Adaptability through negotiation and collaboration."

Constantine also described a pattern that is more common in Asian cultures; a **synchronous** family. Family members have a deep sense of connection, as if they are all branches of the same tree. Harmony and tranquility are valued; people think alike. There is a strong emphasis on non-verbal communication and empathy. A motto might be "Harmony through empathy." When I asked Japanese and U.S. students about their family type, Open and Closed were often chosen in both cultures. Japanese students also often chose Synchronous, and almost never chose Random. U.S. students did the opposite, choosing Random but rarely Synchronous.

In the research project, families made symbolic pictures of their family which included boundary markers. Some families included a boundary around the entire family, others did not. Families also differed as to who was included in the family; a few included friends of the children. Some, particularly Japanese families, included grandparents within the family boundary. One U.S. family depicted a grandfather as on top of the boundary, saying he disturbed their boundary.

There are also boundaries within the family. Some individuals are loners, keeping mostly to themselves. There are also groups. One of the children might put a boundary around themselves and a friend. In our research, one mother put multiple boundary markers around herself, saying "That's me when I'm depressed. No one can get to me."

Family patterns vary by culture, also by religion, ethnicity and the parents' experiences growing up. Different family patterns are adaptive in different contexts. If I'm raising my children in a very dangerous neighborhood, I will want a closed family boundary and tight control, in order to keep them safe. If the neighborhood is safe, I can lighten up and allow more exploration outside of the family.

In our study, Japanese families were more likely to place a boundary around the whole family than were U.S. families. And Japanese fathers were more likely to have an individual boundary, separating them to some extent from the rest of the family. In both Japan and the United States, a boundary around the two parents was included in about half of the family pictures. And parent-child boundaries were common in both cultures. I'll discuss this in more detail in chapter 8, Across Cultures.

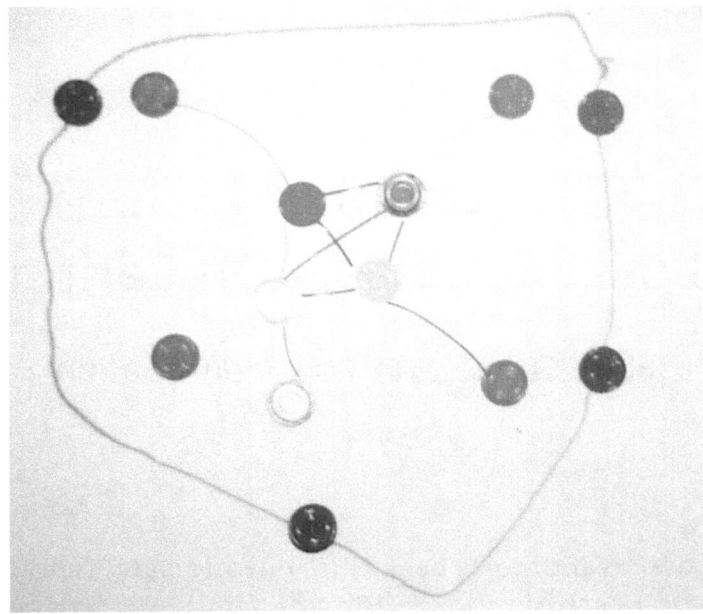

Disturbed Boundary (U.S. picture). The dog is in the picture four times, connected to each of family members because they all feel connected to him. The chips on the top of the boundary are Grampa. He lives with family and drinks all the time. They said he disturbs their boundary.

Chapter 4
Love: Emphasis On Caring

High Connection; Low Individuation

N ow I want to get back to connection and individuation by describing four different families, starting with a family that scored high on connection but low on individuation. Families scoring high on connection have a warm, loving atmosphere. Children feel secure. They experience themselves as trusted and they trust others. Families low on individuation don't value individuality; don't acknowledge each person's individual ideas and feelings. Thus, they tend to be uncomfortable with disagreement. In a family scoring high on connection and low on individuation, there may be an unspoken family rule that "If you disagree with me you don't love me." This would make them uncomfortable with the revealed difference exercise because the exercise by its nature highlights disagreements. In the family I'm describing, anxiety tended to increase as the revealed difference exercise progressed. Family members wanted always to agree, even if someone had to change their answer when they didn't really change their mind. There was no in depth discussion of different opinions. This family's laughter was scored as often anxious, defensive (low individuation) <u>and</u> often warm, responsive (high connection).

Coders listening to the family interaction made the following comments:

- Family members appeared to genuinely care for each other.
- Lots of laughing, especially when expressing negative feelings.
- Family members could express differences of opinion, but always laughing.
- Their affect didn't match their behavior – laughter with disagreement.
- They did not argue their points, were easily swayed, and easily changed their minds.
- Mother spoke for all of the children.
- They did the revealed difference exercise very fast – hurried to get   everybody's say, then voted and quickly moved on to the next item.
- Any disagreement was blamed on the wording of the item.
- Lots of "we" statements, "we think," "we believe."
- Covert conflict seemed high; conflict wasn't allowed to be out in the open.
- There was a rigid family boundary; no mention of friends except for one daughter being "in love."

This family might seek out counseling or therapy when they have adolescents who are seeking more independence, or around some other issue that seems to disrupt the family's need to be always in agreement with each other. A therapist might use a "both, and" approach, enriching the family's worldview: love and respect, closeness and acknowledgement. You can have both; you can be respectful of differences and at the same time maintain closeness. You can love omeone and also disagree with them. If the family seems fearful of disagreement, talking about this openly might support constructive change. What do family members fear might happen if anger is openly expressed? What memories do the parents have from childhood that taught them that disagreements are dangerous?

For immigrant families the struggle may be balancing traditional culture with assimilation to the new culture. The home culture might be more focused on respect for authority, consensus about values and rules for behavior. The family boundary may be closed. Perhaps the children are being pulled towards a more individualistic pattern, desiring western style independence, wanting a more open family boundary, and this is threatening to the parents. Discussion of cultural differences, with a focus on how to incorporate the benefits and strengths of each culture, can often be the key to constructive change.

Chapter 5
Respect: Emphasis On Individuality

High Individuation; Low Connection

O ver much of the child's early years, the parent is focused on meeting the child's attachment needs. However, just as people have a need to be cherished and nurtured, they also have a need to be autonomous and effective. As toddlers begin to be capable of independent action, most parents partially refocus their caregiving on the child's needs for autonomy and effectiveness. Individuation is a prominent developmental process in adolescence and young adulthood. To the extent that parents promote a family system where members are encouraged to think for themselves, speak for themselves, and accept others' differences, children develop their capacity for autonomous action and learn how to direct their efforts effectively toward mastering the environment. Even the experience of conflict, in the right context, can be positive, assisting in identity formation, the development of conflict resolution skills and assertive behavior.

Individuation increases as the child's assertion of ideas and feelings is met by acknowledgement and validation by parents and others. Comfort with individuality and differences supports a more complex self-concept, a personal identity, along with personal autonomy. To the extent that autonomy needs are prioritized, family members will be encouraged to think for themselves, speak for themselves, and accept others' individuality. Children will develop a clear and unique personal identity and a capacity for autonomous action.

The family being described here scored high on individuation, but low on connection. They found the revealed difference exercise to be fun. It was comfortable for them to acknowledge and discusses different ideas from different people. Family members tended to explain their comments. When they were challenged, they were open to further discussion. However, this family lacked a sense of togetherness and was described by coders as somewhat cold, somewhat sad, with little use of joking or humor. One daughter said her feelings were often hurt by what family members said. When making the family picture, the family tried to incorporate everyone's opinion into the picture; each person had an individual boundary.

Coder comments included the following:
- Good negotiations; good problem-solving and conflict resolution skills
- All family members were respected and listened to.
- Very calm, all were verbal.
- They critiqued others' opinions – very detail oriented.
- Wanted to talk and talk and talk about details.
- Family members were very attentive, but not necessarily supportive.
- Affect was neutral; there was not a sense of warmth.
- Parents defended the lack of togetherness (of which they were aware) by saying that the kids were teenagers.

What would lead a family like this one to seek counseling or therapy? Sadness or a lack of joy perhaps. A family member may be depressed; family members are not good at focusing on emotional needs. Perhaps one of the children grows up and finds difficulty in a relationship where their partner wants more intimacy, warmth, and holding. Therapy can give family members the opportunity to learn an emotional language and take the risk of sharing feelings. One approach might be to teach parents about the importance of attachment for humans. Another approach would be to explore parental experiences of connection in their families growing up. Help a mate learn to listen and hold and comfort – and focus less on fixing or solving. Encourage hugs; practice in the therapy session. People who don't talk about feelings could be given a feeling chart (a list or pictures of a large variety of feelings), and each day they are asked to point to a feeling and tell others when they experienced that feeling. Being high on individuation is a great strength and, with time and practice, people who feel more shut down emotionally, or who "don't do hugs," can learn to connect in a more loving way.

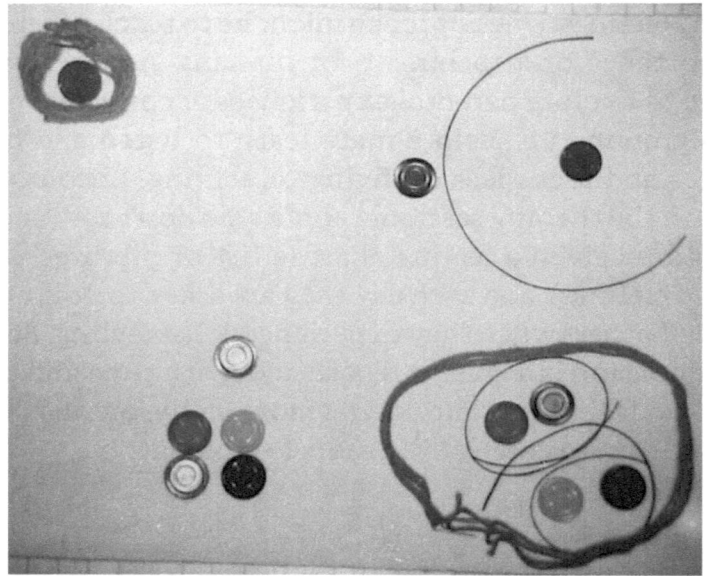

Depressed Mom (U.S. picture). The four family members are in the family boundary at the bottom right. In the upper right there's a black line between a son and his uncle because they don't get along. The lower left hand corner shows the family with the dog. They said that the dog came into the family to bring them all together. That's Mom up in the left-hand corner, with lots of boundary markers. She said that when she's depressed no one can get to her.

Chapter 6
Love and Respect

High Connection; High Individuation

S ome people, including some family researchers, conceive of connection and individuation as the extreme ends of one scale. The more connection in a relationship, the less individuated it is and vice versa. I mentioned the tendency of some people to associate affection and agreement. "If you disagree with me, you don't love me." Another fear might be that being very close with you means I don't have my own space; I don't have room for my own ideas and feelings. This way of thinking about connection and individuation misses the way the two processes can support one another. Luckily many families find a way to have both close connection and strong individuation. A high connection/high individuation family is warm and close, <u>and</u> each person is respected as an individual with ideas and feelings that others validate. Validation is when you experience having the right to think and feel the way you do, and you allow others that same right. It is not about agreement. I can love you and disagree with you at the same time. And I can listen, understand and validate you even when I disagree.

A family in our study that scored high on both characteristics looked very healthy, flexible and cohesive, very supportive and very good at communication. They were able to express sad and anxious feelings and scored high on the use of humor. As the discussion of differences progressed, acknowledgement and laughter increased. They were described as demonstrating clear points of view, asking for others' opinions, understanding others' feelings, and responding relevantly to each other.

This family made a somewhat complex family picture, showing individual and family boundaries, relationships between individuals inside and outside of the family, and relationships between the parents and each of the children.

Coders comments included the following:
- The parents have an alliance and so do the kids.
- The family used humor to show warmth and caring.
- People were curious about others' reasons for answering as they did.
- It was OK to disagree, recognizing that different family members have different experiences.
- When they disagreed, they could see each other's perspectives.
- All had a voice.
- They equally shared opinions and perspectives, and often changed their minds.
- The family displayed a supportive, loving, playful, sense of togetherness.
- It was OK not to reach agreement.

You might think a family like this would never seek therapy, but I've found that healthier families often seek help when they hit a rough patch, for instance when children are entering adolescence, or a parent loses a job or is going to work for the first time. A family might choose to talk with a counselor or therapist after a crisis or loss. Important therapeutic behaviors could include providing an empathic ear, helping family members see that their experience is normal, giving the family members information about how others have dealt with the issue they are facing. These families bring many strengths that a therapist can highlight, access, and help them utilize.

Chapter 7
Neither Nor
Low Connection; Low Individuation

This family did not have strengths in either connection or individuation. They were described by coders as unhealthy, rigid and disengaged, with poor communication. They described themselves as low on organization and very low on control. During the revealed difference task they were both sad and anxious, did not acknowledge each other, and showed little humor. They avoided actual discussion of their differences. Individuals were seen as very unreceptive to other family members' statements. They left little room for others' input, used derogatory or criticizing remarks and tone, and tended to monologue without acknowledging others' attempts to speak. The family appeared to pull back from the task because it was scary. When making the family picture, family members cooperated to some extent, but ended up making three different pictures because of their inability to agree on a common picture.

Coders' comments included the following:
- There seemed to be some underlying conflict between the parents which wasn't being expressed.
- Dad led the family discussion which was disorganized and disorderly.
- Individual differences were not clearly established.

- The whole family seemed tense when together.
- It sounded like the children were in control of the family.
- No laughter.
- Weak family boundary; there was a sense that the teenagers would just like to get out.
- There was overt conflict between Mom and one daughter.
- Dad stressed verbally that he could only speak for himself, but constantly spoke for the other family members.
- Much anger was expressed.
- There was mention of physical discipline, hitting.
- Family members had many opposing ideas, but they didn't seem to be able to discuss or resolve them.
- Lots of items were marked "no agreement" during the revealed difference exercise.
- Even when the conflict was openly expressed, they didn't resolve the problem because no one listened to anyone else – they just talked.

This family might find their way to therapy via a referral by a school or court. Strong support and direction from a counselor or therapist would probably be helpful. Identifying concrete goals and teaching communication and conflict management skills could also be useful. Exploring expectations and past experiences concerning conflict or disagreement is another possibility. A discussion of a disagreement with some guidance from the therapist would be a way to allow the family to practice the sharing of differences with positive rather than negative consequences. The family might then be able to follow through with homework. It might be possible to address attachment issues between the couple, or in parent-child relationships, encouraging more affection. Looking back at the families the parents grew up in could help people get some perspective on their current situation. They learned their way of being, and they can learn something new.

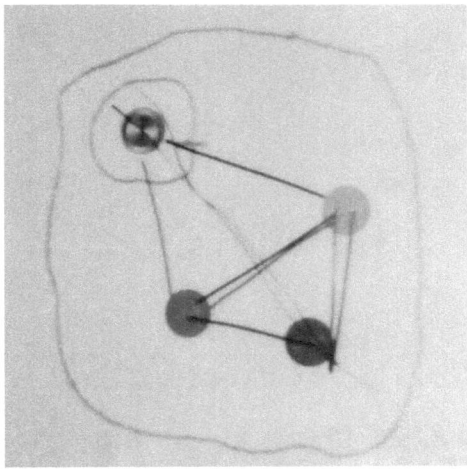

Distant Dad (Japanese picture). Mother and children are close. Father has an individual boundary. He's somewhat distant from the others.

Chapter 8

Across Cultures: Japan And The U. S.

I n the mid 1980s my family and I traveled to Japan where my husband and I continued the research on families. I was fortunate to come to Japan when the family therapy movement was taking off, so I was able to teach family therapy in addition to doing the family interviews. I learned a lot about Japanese families from my Japanese colleagues.

For families in the United States, the marriage tends to be considered the center or foundation of the family. Two people marry, forming a new family. They are responsible for helping to meet each other's needs. In a healthy family, the marriage partners' relationship supports and sustains their ongoing commitment to one another. With the addition of new members into the family, the marital relationship expands to support effective parenting. American children usually sleep separately from parents, even when very young; the couple has their privacy.

The Japanese experience historically reflected a different pattern. Traditionally in Japan, the marriage was primarily seen as a partnership for raising children rather than a personal relationship meant to fulfill the psychological needs of the mates. Two families were joined in marriage for the purpose of continuing a family line; most marriages were arranged marriages rather than love matches. The woman left her family to join the husband's family; the mother took care of the husband and the children. Japanese children usually sleep with or near a parent. The blood bonds of parent and child are viewed as naturally stronger and more basic than the marital relationship. Historically, the mother-oldest son relationship was of particular importance.

Another cultural difference is that Americans have traditionally placed a higher value on individuation, Japanese on connection. Americans are more likely to nurture individuality in children and to value individual autonomy. Japanese place a primary value on being able to rely on others, on people caring for each other. Japanese traditional culture remained fairly strong at the time we were doing our research, although younger generations seemed to be moving toward placing more value on individuality. They also were often preferring a choice of mates based on love. It is important to note that both Japanese and Americans value both connection and individuation. While there are noticeable differences, there is also a fundamental agreement. The difference is a matter of emphasis.

We interviewed a sample of Japanese families in the mid-1980s. Structured home interviews in Japan, as in the U.S., included a projective exercise in which families made pictures of the family. The instructions for the picture were to create a picture of the family, everyone working together. As in the U.S., there were different colored circles to represent people, red and black lines to put between individuals to show similarity or difference, and boundary markers to show individuals who were separate or pairs or groups of people who belonged together.

Family patterns, as presented in these pictures, were compared for the U. S. and Japan. We expected the marital relationship to be closer in the U.S., the mother-eldest son relationship closer in Japan. We also expected more paternal grandmothers to be included in Japan. The results were not entirely as we predicted. A number of themes were similar for families in both cultures. In both there was a tendency to see the parents/ mates as a unit, and to see them as close to each other. There was also a greater likelihood, in both cultures, of including grand-mothers in the family (compared with grandfathers). And sons were likely to be closest to fathers; daughters, to mothers.

Marriage appeared to be based more on a personal re-lationship in the U.S., with mates seen as more similar to each other than in Japan. Japanese families were more likely to make multiple family pictures. These showed different characteristics (personality, behavior, sports, food preferences) or times (morn-ing, evening meal, etc.). The experience of the family depended on the context. Japanese fathers were more likely to be seen as isolated than were U.S. fathers. Japanese mothers, compared with Japanese fathers, were depicted as more connected with children. This was consistent with a common Japanese pattern in which the husband is away from home a great deal of the time with work.

In our relationships with Japanese families and col-leagues, we developed a deeper awareness of the importance of nurturing mutual dependency and connection among family members. This Japanese focus on connection and interdepend-ence compares with a stronger focus on individuation and indi-viduality in the U.S. In one study, we asked men, women, boys and girls in both cultures to rank the relative importance of various family traits. Items used to measure individuation were (1) each family member is respected as an individual with their own ideas and feelings; (2) each family member is actively encouraged to develop autonomy and individuality (or to "make their own de-cisions" in the children's questionnaire); and (3) there is tolerance for real differences of opinion among family members. Connec-tion in the family was also measured by three items: (1) warm, loving, caring atmosphere in the family; (2) people can really trust each other and depend on each other; and (3) dependency needs are expressed and cared for in healthy ways (or "harmony among family members" in the children's questionnaire). Other items focused on communication, problem solving and family roles.

Looking at the results of the rankings:

- Children ranked connection, as compared with individuation, as more
important than did the adults
- Girls ranked connection as more important than did the boys.
- The Americans (adults and children) valued individuation more than did
the Japanese.
- For Japanese, adults and children, and for American women and girls, the most important item was "warm, loving, caring atmosphere in the family." For American boys and men, the most important item was "Each family member is respected as an individual with their own ideas and feelings."
- Looking at the adult answers, there was a significant difference between the valuing of connection by Japanese and American men. Japanese men valued connection most, more than Japanese or American women and much more than the American men.

When researchers do cross-cultural studies, there's a tendency to focus on differences. However, when studying families in Japan and the United States, we were looking for both similarities and differences. It's important to remember that the differences we found in cultures are differences in degree rather than in kind, and to remember that there are large areas of similarity. In the study just discussed, when we asked people to describe their ideal family, both Japanese and Americans valued both connection and individuation. It's also important to remember that cultures are constantly evolving – the Japanese becoming more individualistic; Americans, perhaps more valuing of connection. In some ways, then, we may be becoming more similar.

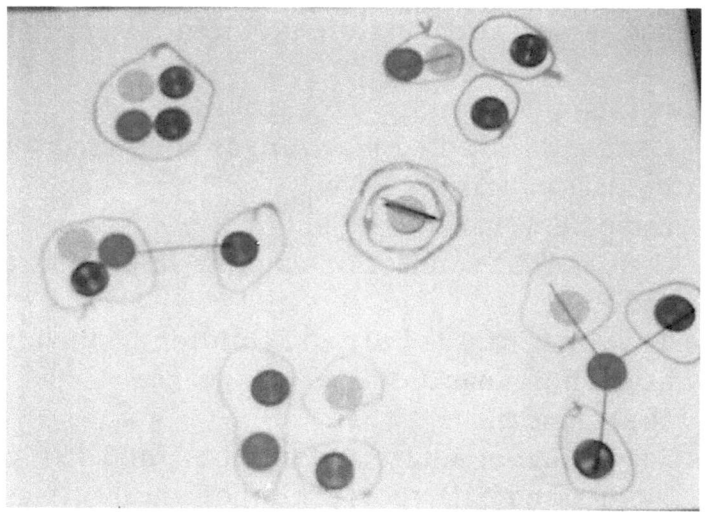

Deep Connection (Japanese picture). This is the family at different times. Upper left is on holiday; upper right is afternoon snack (mother and oldest daughter together). Lower right, how they are in the morning (Mom's in the center). Middle-left -- how they are at dinner time – Dad's alone; he's never home. The center image shows a deep connection; family members are all together, the circles are stacked.

Chapter 9

Triangulation and Personal Maturity

Social scientists have often noted the instability of a relationship in the face of conflict or stress. You may have noticed it too. Those in a relationship may address instability in a number of ways, depending on the culture, the history of the relationship, and individual problem-solving skills. One response to conflict or stress would simply be a cooling off period. Another approach, as a two-person relationship becomes uncomfortable, is for a third person to be drawn in to stabilize things, a process called "triangulation." Triangulation is ubiquitous in human relationships. If I'm in an uncomfortable relationship with a friend, I may talk to another friend to complain or try to get help. In the family any individual -- parent, child or grandparent -- may be "triangled." A common example would be a parent pulled in to resolve a conflict between two children.

When tension arises in a marriage, triangulation of a child might occur to stabilize and protect the marital relationship. Parents, for example, may avoid tension in their relationship by focusing together on a child's or adolescent's problem. If Eileen is in trouble at school, for instance, the parents might avoid thinking about their own difficulties and instead focus together on how to help Eileen. This might help the couple make the marriage more stable, less threatened. One child in therapy responded to my question "What would happen if you got better, if your problem went away?" Response: "My parents would divorce." If parents bring a child to see a therapist, the therapist might explore issues in the marriage as a way of helping the child. If the marital relationship improves, the child's concerns may also subside, as the parents no longer need a distraction.

Another way to involve a child would be to pull the child or adolescent into a coalition with one of the parents: Mom complains about Dad to their adolescent son, for instance. Either way the parents can be said to have triangled their child. The particular relationship pattern can be different for each child in the family. One child pulled in to "save" the parents' marriage can leave others free to develop without having to take on this responsibility.

Triangulation of a child may lead to a lower level of health for the child because it means that behavior toward the child is based on parental needs rather than on the child's own needs. This is a kind of invalidation or lack of respect for the child's needs. An idea we wished to test in our research was that triangulation would be associated with lower levels of personal maturity in adolescents because their own needs would be less likely to be responded to appropriately. We expected triangulating parents would become less able to respond to a child based on the child's needs, acting instead based on their own needs to protect the marriage.

To explore this idea, we measured the triangulation of adolescents, in each family identifying the most triangled. Thus, in a family where there was no triangulation, the most triangled child would have a very low score on triangulation. Then we looked at two patterns. The first pattern was the relationship between couples avoiding discussing conflicts in the marriage and the amount of triangulation. The second was the relationship between amount of triangulation and the personal maturity of the adolescent.

How did we measure personal maturity? We used a measure developed by Jane Loevinger called "ego development." Our sample tended to be at one of two levels of ego development on Loevinger's measure. We'll call these "social" and "conscientious." At the social stage people have developed beyond the childish stage of simply being self-protective, seeking to gain rewards and avoid pain. Children move into the social stage when they have some ability to trust others. Trusting others, I feel myself to be part of a group; I follow the rules because they are the rules of my group. I stop at the light because that's the law. I tell my children "In our family, we --- don't hit each other, tell the truth, etc." If you ask a girl why she volunteers to fix sandwiches at the homeless shelter, or why she tutors a younger child, she might say, "Because I'm a Girl Scout."

The next stage, conscientious, means I've thought more deeply about my personal values and beliefs, and I act based on those beliefs. That is, rather than doing things because that's the way I have been told, how my group says I am supposed to behave, instead I guide my behavior more by my own principles. I volunteer at the food bank because I personally believe in helping others who are part of my community. When my teenager is thinking about what to do in a difficult situation, I might ask her to think about what her values are, what kind of a person she wants to be. More mature adolescents, those with higher levels of ego development, will be more likely to make decisions based thoughtfully on personal values rather than by simply following group or family rules.

As expected, parents who had difficulty discussing their disagreements with each other during the revealed difference exercise were more likely to have a triangled adolescent. And in both Japan and the U.S., the greater the triangulation, the lower the personal maturity of a triangled adolescent daughter. More triangled girls were less likely to have reached the conscientious stage of personal maturity. Unfortunately, we couldn't do this study for sons because our sample of sons was too small. As you may remember, we had selected families with 2 or 3 children because one child was an adolescent daughter – who might have a sister(s) or brother(s) -- so we ended up with many more girls than boys in our study.

Chapter 10

Healthy Families
Healthy Kids

*Some Family Characteristics of More
or Less Healthy Adolescents*

At the start of our study in the mid-70s, we had visited three high schools in one school district, looking for 16-17-year-old girls who lived in families with two parents and two or three children. With their parents' permission, these girls completed a number of questionnaires which allowed us to measure their social and psychological health and their personal maturity. We then asked families to participate in home interviews. It's important to note that the families of the very least healthy girls tended to decline the interview.

During the home interview, we also asked about parental education and measured the parents' personal maturity.

For both girls and parents, personal maturity was measured using Jane Loevinger's ego development measure described in the previous chapter. In our sample, parents with more personal maturity and higher levels of education were likely to create healthier families -- loving, connected families in which people also respected each other as individuals. That is, families scoring relatively high in both connection and individuation.

We then looked at how the families of the healthiest and least healthy girls in our sample answered a questionnaire describing their family. Compared to families of the less healthy girls, the families of the more healthy girls described themselves as flexible and trusting. Family members were said to be allowed and encouraged to act openly and to express their feelings. They were encouraged to be assertive and self-sufficient – to think things out for themselves. They described themselves as helpful and supportive of each other. Family members of the less healthy adolescents described families where order and organization were of primary importance. These families were more likely to be organized in a rigid way with rules and procedures; family members were more likely to be described as ordering each other around.

Families of the healthier girls (compared with families of the less healthy girls in the sample) were more likely to agree with statements like:

+ We are allowed to come and go as we want in our family.
+ There are few rules to follow.
+ We can say what we want and are rarely ordered around.
+ Family members support each other, back each other up.
+ We have a feeling of togetherness in our family.

Families of the less healthy girls (compared with families of the healthier girls) were more likely to agree with statements like:

+ In our family, it's "work before play."
+ We can't get away with anything in our family.
+ We have to keep our rooms neat.
+ People sometimes hit each other.
+ It's important to always be on time in our family.

They were also much more likely to say that dishes were done immediately after eating!

We also looked at triangulation of the more and less healthy adolescents. Triangulation, as discussed in the previous chapter, is the tendency for parents to involve a child in order to avoid having to focus on uncomfortable marital issues. The child may be pulled into a relationship with one parent against the other; or the child may be "distanced" from the parents by getting into trouble. The idea is that when a child is triangled, it helps parents avoid facing concerns in their marriage, thus relieving pressure on the marriage. We found what you might expect. The less healthy adolescents were more likely to be triangled, either distanced, or in a coalition with one parent against the other. Their siblings were not triangled. This suggests that when one child is triangled, other children are free to develop based on their own needs rather than by meeting parental needs.

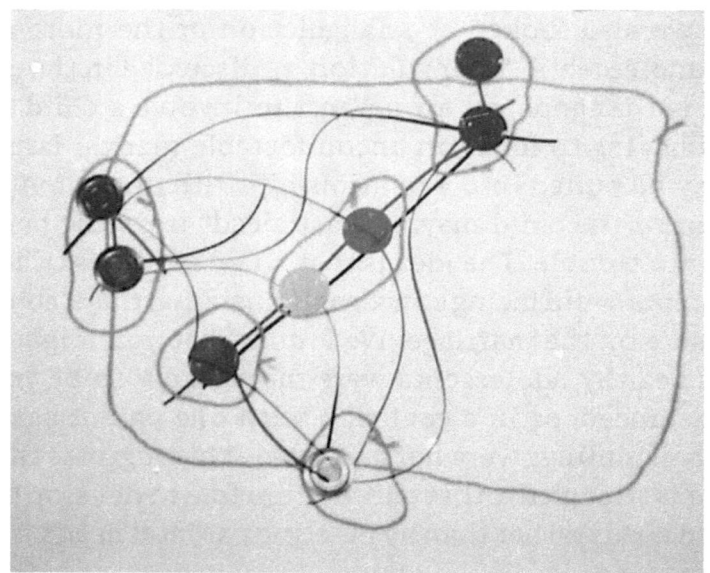

Friends (U.S. picture). Mom and Dad are in the middle. Grandparents are on the left border. Friends of son and daughter are mostly outside the family boundary.

Chapter 11

Close Family
Close Friends

Beginning at birth, family relationships and interactions affect the personal development of children, their sense of security in relationships, their ability to trust, and the extent to which they feel loved or cherished. These experiences can nurture self-esteem and resilience in the face of hardship. Likewise, being listened to, being praised, being taught that when you try for goals there is often failure but it's important to keep going. Everything from table manners to expectations about sleep, ways of resolving (or not resolving) disagreement and conflict, expectations about how people treat each other – all of these affect the personal development of the child. They help the growing child build an understanding of how the world works, how people treat each other, how close relationships can be expected to be, whether or not people can be trusted. The family experiences become like a map – a set of understandings and expectations about how the world works.

Family experiences naturally affect how children relate to others outside of the family, including their peers. The child's map is developed based on family experiences; it is like a blueprint of relationship patterns. Children use their maps to understand and engage the world outside of the family. The map becomes the prism through which they see the world – their expectations of what other people are like, their ideas about how to behave. And when they act in the world as they perceive it, they are likely to have their views validated, in part because they seek out people and contexts that feel familiar to them. A child who has a secure attachment to parents or other caregivers will expect that others will be trustworthy and caring. If a child has become anxious about whether or not people will be there for them, whether or not others are trustworthy, they will approach the world with caution. They may be drawn to others who are also cautions, or by being cautions, evoke caution in others, and thus reduce closeness. If they have seen parents and siblings accept differences and demonstrate good conflict resolution skills, they will try to practice these skills with others and may be surprised if they run into apparently irresolvable conflict with their peers.

The family, then, will naturally influence how the children create and experience their peer relationships. And those relationships, in turn, are important, especially during adolescence. In one analysis, we focused on the relationship between family patterns and friendship patterns. To start the research we gave questionnaires to high school students that included questions about who their friends were. This allowed us to come up with some friendship measures for the girls in our sample. One measure was how many friend choices the girl received; another was the percent of people she chose as friends who chose her back. In this way we were able to come up with a picture of her friendship network – the closeness of her friendship ties.

When we coded the family interaction, one thing we evaluated was the degree of closeness among family members. At one extreme were families which were very close, very involved with each other; at the other extreme were families in which family members seemed isolated or disconnected from each other. The healthier families were toward the close end, but not all the way – close and caring, but not in each other's hair so to speak. Then we looked at the relationship between the girls' families and the girls' friendship networks. The result was that girls with closer family relationships tended to form closer relationships with friends. The closer the family, the closer the friendship network – until we got to the extremely close families. In extremely close families, the girls were less close with friends than were the girls in the next to closest families.

We interpret this result as showing that children become comfortable with the level of closeness experienced in their families. The family relationships evolve into their map of how relationships work. When they are outside the family, they tend choose friends with whom they can recreate the familiar pattern. Close family, close friends; disconnected family relationships, disconnected friendship patterns. What I know, what I'm used to, I expect; I create and nurture the pattern I am familiar with. This is true, of course, with other family experiences. The family is where we learn how the world works, what is and what can be – our understanding of how things are. We use this understanding, this map, to help us navigate the world outside the family.

Chapter 12

When the Kids Grow Up

What happened when the adolescents grew up? Did growing up in healthier families, connected and individuated families, influence who they were as adults? We interviewed the adolescents in the families we studied when they were adults, about 25 years after the original family interview. The children who grew up in healthier families were doing better personally, that is, they had higher levels of wellbeing as adults. This was true both in the U.S. and in Japan.

We measured wellbeing using a questionnaire developed by Carol Ryff, a questionnaire that measures several aspects of wellbeing. One aspect is the **relationships** we have with others. Positive relationships can nurture and enrich our lives; lack of meaningful relationships can leave us feeling lonely and sad. Would you agree or disagree with the statement "I have warm relationships with other people"? How about, "I have some close friends."

Ryff's questionnaire also measures **autonomy.** Autonomy is about self-determination, being one's own person, rather than being under the strong influence of someone else who is exercising authority. It has to do with liberty and freedom. A person feeling autonomous would be unlikely to say that they are strongly influenced by the opinions of others. They would be more likely to say that they are following their own choices about what they are doing on a day-to-day basis.

Another characteristic that's been identified as part of wellbeing is **growth**. This is the feeling that opportunities exist for learning and becoming, and the individual takes advantage of those opportunities. The opposite of growth would be feeling that everything meaningful or valuable in life, if it ever existed, is now past. A person might say that they have given up trying to make any improvements in their lives. People experiencing a life of growth might say that their life has been an experience of learning and growing.

A sense of **purpose** in life is another characteristic often associated with wellbeing and measured by Ryff. Likewise, people with a greater wellbeing often feel a greater sense of **mastery** over what happens in their lives. The demands of daily living are manageable. People feel they are mostly in charge of their lives.

Finally, wellbeing is defined as including a higher level of **self-acceptance.** People like themselves. When they look back over their lives, they will say that they are happy with how things have gone.

In our study, healthy families led to higher levels of wellbeing for former adolescents, even 25 years after the family interview. Particularly, in the U.S. sample, connection in the adolescent family was associated with self-acceptance and positive relationships at midlife; individuation was associated with autonomy.

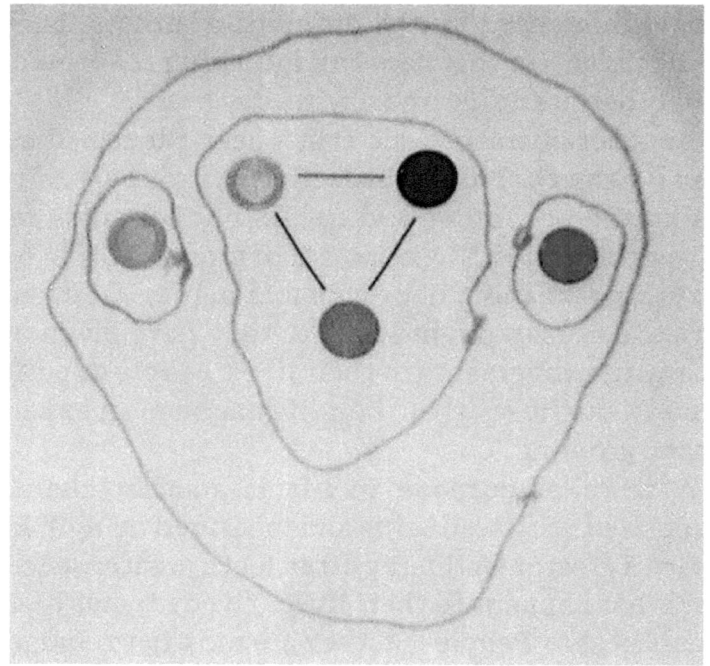

Internal Boundaries (Japanese picture). Mother, father, and oldest son are inside a common boundary; daughter and younger son each have their own personal boundaries. Everyone is inside the family boundary.

Chapter 13

Adult Child-Elder Parent Relationships

F amily can be a major support system for people of all ages. About 25 years after the original home interview, we did telephone interviews with the adult former adolescents and with their then elder parents. One thing we looked at was the relationships between the adult children and their elder parents. We also looked at the effect of those relationships on the elders' health and wellbeing. Much of the research on adult child – elder parent relationships shows that caregiving and support are reciprocal until parents are very elderly. At that point, the caregiving begins to go primarily from the adult children to the elder parents. In recent decades, relationships between parents and their adult children have become even more important to elders as a result of increased longevity.

The adult children's relationship to their elder parents was measured by whether or not the elders felt loved and respected by their adult children. <u>Affection and support</u> were measured by whether or not the elder parent felt that the adult child was paying attention to them, helped them when they needed help, and whether or not the adult child could be depended on. <u>Respect</u> was measured by the elder saying whether or not they felt respected as an individual by their adult child, whether they had mutual respect, and whether the adult child saw them "as they really are." <u>Wellbeing</u> was measured using Ryff's instrument described in the previous chapter; that is autonomy, mastery, personal growth, positive relations with others, purpose in life and self-acceptance. As usual, the health of the <u>family system</u> was measured by connection and individuation.

In our sample, elder mothers had more contact with adult children than did elder fathers, a common finding by others. Elder mothers also reported more positive relationships with their adult children than did elder fathers. Both elder parents also reported more contact with adult daughters than with adult sons and more positive relationships with adult daughters than with adult sons. This was true both in the U.S. and in Japan.

The research supported the significant influence of family health when the children were growing up on later life relationships between adult children and their elder parents. Our results suggested that family connection led to more respect for elder fathers in both the U.S. and Japan. U.S. elder fathers also reported more affection from adult children when the family was higher in individuation. Looking at the U.S. data, midlife adults from more connected, more individuated families maintained good relationships with their parents. That is, a healthier family during the adult children's adolescence led to more affection and more respect between the adult child and the elder parents 25 years later. Positive relationships led to more frequent contact between the adult children and the elder parents. Positive relationships with their adult children also led to higher levels of wellbeing for the elder parents; this was true for both mothers and fathers. For the elder fathers, frequent contact with their adult children also led to better physical health.

Many studies have shown that qualities of the adult child – elder parent relationship are critical for issues of elder health and wellbeing. What's special here is that those relationships can be traced back to family connection and individuation when the children were adolescents. Family health during adolescence was found to affect the adult children's affection, respect, and support for their elder parents. This relationship, in turn, influenced the elder parents' wellbeing.

For our sample, frequency of contact with children was particularly important for fathers – both for their wellbeing and for their physical health. Some research suggests that marital relationships may also be particularly important for men, that, in the generation we studied, men experienced a stronger benefit from marriage than women. Also, that parental marriage results in closer ties (more frequent contact) between adult children and their fathers. In our study, too, intact marriages resulted in more frequent contact between adult children and their fathers. Our data suggested that contact with adult children may be more important for fathers than for mothers. It could be that mothers in our sample were more likely to have social supports outside of the family, whereas the men relied more heavily on their families for social support.

Chapter 14

Generation to Generation

F amilies have profound effects for individual family members throughout life. This analysis addressed the question
of whether or not early family effects continue into the
next generation by influencing the families created by the adult
children. We also looked at the adult children's ability to make
specific changes when they created their own families, whether
or not they were able to create healthier families than the ones
they grew up in.

We interviewed the families of the adult children when
they had adolescents of their own. Families in the two generations participated in the same home interview. Both were
interviewed at the time of the family life cycle, when there
were adolescents in the family. As you will recall, during home
interviews family members completed a questionnaire describing their family. They then discussed differences of opinion about
the family and jointly created a "picture" of their family. All
families were coded for connection and individuation using the
scales described in chapter 2. In addition to the coding, we also
looked at how the two generations of families described themselves on the questionnaire used for their revealed difference discussion.

Continuity

Both family members' reports and coded measures from the family interaction process supported a continuity between family system traits in the original families and those of the next generation's families. As you might expect, a healthier family growing up was associated with a healthier family in the next generation, the families of the adult children. Respect and validation (individuation) in the families growing up was associated with less conflict in the families created by the adult children. This was true for both mothers and fathers (the former daughters and sons). For fathers, connection in their families growing up was associated both with more love (connection) and more respect (individuation) in the family in which they were the father.

Based on the families' answers on the questionnaire, we found that greater levels of conflict in families growing up was associated with greater levels of conflict in the adult children's families. We also found evidence that, for mothers, if there were higher levels of expressing feelings in the family they grew up in, there were also higher levels of expressing feelings in the family in which they were the mothers.

Change

When we asked the adult children what they wanted to change from their original families, those who wanted a change focused on three areas: connection, individuation, and conflict.

Examples of intended changes for connection (love, affection):
- More loving and honest
- Be more caring to my children
- More involved in the things that they do
- Always tell each child I love them
- Show affection on a daily basis
- Be more physically affectionate

Examples of intended changes for individuation (respect, validation):
- Children can voice their opinions to adults
- Open communication between all of us
- Let kids make own decision more
- Encourage my kids to be more independent
- I try to allow each one to be who they are
- Honor individuality

Examples of intended changes for conflict:
- Don't fight and not talk
- I want them to see less conflict and anger
- No hitting
- Manage anger; not have an insane temper like my father
- No spanking
- Not so quick to anger

It was impressive to find that both mothers and fathers who wanted to create something different, were able to purposely change family characteristics – to create their own families to be healthier than what they knew as children. The intent for less conflict led to more affection. The desire for more affection led to more respect. Fathers' intentions to create more respectful families led to more respect and less conflict. These results were from the coding of the family discussions during the revealed difference exercise. We then looked at how the parents themselves described the families they grew up in and their current families. If the intent of the parents was to create families that had less conflict than those in which they grew up, they were able to do that. This was true for both mothers and fathers.

Thus, we found continuity between the families the parents grew up in and the families they created. We also found that when parents set out to create something better, they were able to make changes in the positive direction. They were not bound to recreate exactly what they had experienced growing up. The family I grew up in affects the family I help create as a parent. However, I can affect some change for the better. This research supports the idea that when parents focus on particular characteristics that they wish to change from the families they grew up in, it enhances their success in making those changes.

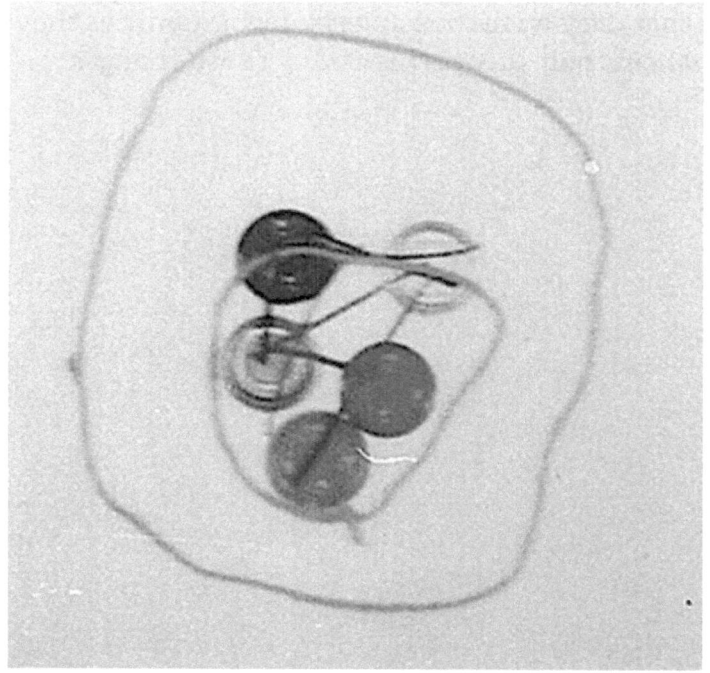

Growing Up (U.S. picture). All family members are inside a large family boundary, but the two older kids are halfway out of the small family boundary. They are teenagers, in the process of becoming more independent, separating from the small family circle, but still inside of the larger circle.

Chapter 15

Marriage Improves in Later Life

For the U.S. sample, we were able to study the relationship between marital health in midlife and marital health in later life. Twenty-five years after the first interview, the elder parents were interviewed again in their homes. Of the 99 original couples, we were able to interview 44 who were both still alive and healthy 25 years later -- when they were in their late 60s or early 70s. Only 6 couples had divorced or separated.

During each home interview, at midlife and in later life, couples completed a questionnaire describing their family, then discussed differences of opinion about the family and tried to reach agreement. Marital system connection and individuation were coded from taped discussions using scales like those described in Chapter 2.

We found relationships between midlife and later life marriage as well as evidence of marital quality improving in later life. Connection at midlife was positively related to warmth, support and mutual respect in later life. More affection at midlife was also related to less depression in later life. Mutual respect at midlife was associated with less conflict in later life.

Also, in later life there was an improvement in couples' relationship health. Particularly, in later life there was more warmth and support, more respect for individuality, more comfort with differences, and less covert conflict than there had been earlier at midlife. Thus, our results give us an optimistic picture of long-term marriages. We found no significant change for humor, overt conflict, problem-solving effectiveness, or depression; scores on these qualities remained constant.

We also asked the interviewed couples what they thought was important in order to have a good marriage. A major theme was commitment, the ability to hang in through the rough times. Remember, these were people who grew up during the depression and married after World War II. Many of these couples told us that divorce was simply not an option in their generation. They stressed the importance of trusting one another; it was up to them to make the marriage as good or as bad as it was going to be. "This marriage was going to be it."

Many couples stayed together through very difficult times. And we still saw improved relationships in later life. One couple told me they had had one bad decade, but then things got better. Integrity and the ability to trust one another were also mentioned by over half of the couples interviewed. As one person said, you have to believe that your mate is always going to be honest with you and faithful to you, and you can't expect perfection.

The couples stressed both connection and individuation, affection and respect. You don't have to get along all the time, but you do need to like each other. "Don't marry anyone that you don't basically respect as a person; accept the person for who they are." You also have to respect your mate's time alone and their privacy.

Another focus was similarity and complementarity – and the need for both. One worries; one is playful. One is an optimist, the other a pessimist. It's OK to have different interests; this can enrich the marriage. But some things are important to have in common -- like faith, philosophy of life, morals.

Seventy percent of couples also mentioned something

about communication, problem solving, or compromise, the importance of being open and talking things out. But you don't have to agree all the time. Many talked about the ability to let things go – you can't solve every problem and you don't need to. Finally, humor was mentioned as important to a successful marriage by about a fourth of the couples.

Chapter 16

Family Systems and Family Therapy

Ill of us, in some way or another, are members of families. The family creates a primary reality for children and adolescents as they absorb their family's culture. Models, thought patterns, expectations and meanings absorbed in the family pervade the rest of life, both through filtering our perceptions and through expectations of what is and what can be. Beginning early on a child learns if they are cared for, if the world is safe, if people can be depended on. They carry these expectations throughout life, having them strengthened, challenged or altered to varying degrees through life experiences.

Healthy families contribute to a child's wellbeing. While there are many variations, research by Froma Walsh found certain remarkable similarities in strong resilient families across cultures and ethnicities. Successful families are described as close and caring, respectful of individual autonomy, exhibiting clear, open, spontaneous communication, effective problem solving skills, and spiritual wellbeing.

Therapists working with children in the 1950s began to notice that often if one child was helped, another would become troubled. If all the children got better, then sometimes the parents' marital problems came to the fore. One young boy answered my question "What would happen if you got better, if your problem went away?" His response was: "My parents would divorce." Therapists started talking with parents and whole families, rather than just doing individual therapy with the child, because they realized that whatever was going on with the child probably had something to do with what was going on in the family. The new idea for early family therapists was that helping the child included involving the parents, and helping the family create healthier ways of being.

Family systems theory evolved as a way of looking at the child or adult in the context of their relationships – their role in the family or couple, the family's rules for how to live together. An example of a role would be Mom or Dad – or Oldest Child. Other examples of roles are: the Good Child, the Scapegoat, the Smart One, the Mediator, Heart of the Family, Star, Baby. .... By Family Rule, we mean basically, patterns that the family has – not all rules are conscious. A simple rule might be "If you disagree with me, it means you don't love me." or "If you talk back, you get hit." Or, "In our family we always tell each other the truth." Another example of a rule is "If the tension rises between Mom and Dad, Bobby picks a fight with Susie in order to distract them." A family might not be aware of all these so-called "rules."

Systems researchers and therapists also look at family communication patterns. What you communicate (either verbally or non-verbally) affects others and their response affects you. It goes around and around. Communication can be in "code" because some feelings are uncomfortable. A dad raised in poverty with a fair amount of violence in the neighborhood might not have learned to express warm feelings. He may never say "I love you." Instead he could say, "That dress looks OK." Communication can be invalidating. A child who says, "I hate Susie," might be told "No you don't; we don't hate each other in this family. You're just tired; you need a nap." Sometimes there's a double message – when verbal and non-verbal messages contradict each other. A double message can lead to a double bind – a "damned if you do, damned if you don't" situation. If I come home upset and my husband, David, is watching TV, I could say "I've had a horrible day; please just leave me alone." The double message is that my affect says, "I need help," but my words say, "Leave me alone." ..... Dave could be caught in a double bind. If he comes into the bedroom to help me, I could shout at him to leave; "I told you to leave me alone." If he simply keeps watching TV, I might come out and berate him for not caring about me.

One of the most important concepts in Family Systems Theory is the Family Life Cycle Stage, e.g. "early marriage," or "family with adolescents," or "family in later life." Difficulties often arise when families are moving from one life cycle stage to the next, for instance from a family with young children to a family with adolescents. They may have difficulty adapting new rules. OR one person wants a change, and another does not. A desire to change the system example could be a wife deciding she wants to have a career or get a job when the original "contract" was that the husband was the provider and the wife the homemaker. A death in the family almost always requires a change in the family system. Early on I noticed that many of the families I saw in therapy had had a death in the family within a year of coming in to see me. Therapists often assist the family to create a more effective system for their current needs when things are changing.

Obviously, families with different ethnic backgrounds have different patterns and rules too. How much privacy is considered appropriate will usually vary – people of Italian heritage may tend to keep the doors open; people of Nordic heritage may keep them closed – and knock first. One of my students from a more reserved family once asked another student if she always knocked before entering her child's room. The other student basically said, "Of course not; why would they keep the door closed anyway?" Cultural differences are general differences, of course, and might not apply to a specific family. But usually if you learn more about a family's ethnicity, you can understand them better.

You can also understand a family better if you understand their context. Are they struggling economically? Do they live in the country or the city? Are they living in a war zone? Did the parents grow up during an economic depression? Are they immigrating from a culture with different expectations than the one they are moving into?

System means that all of the parts are interrelated. As members of a family system every member is interconnected. If one changes, all are affected. Like a mobile. Move one piece and the whole pattern shifts. The idea is that to understand an individual, we must understand the systems that individual is a part of. If we try to understand people only as autonomous and disconnected, we can't see the whole picture.

Through time, many things happen to and in a family. As things change, the family adapts, the system recalibrates as the children grow up, also to accommodate new people, death, societal events, good and bad fortune. For many families, a healthier pattern evolves with time. Family connection, family individuation, personal maturity and wellbeing can continue to improve as a result of life experiences that happen both inside and outside of the family. People can learn to love and respect at the same time – let children know they are accepted and loved just as they are. That it's OK to love and respect someone you disagree with.

Family Systems Therapy

How does a family therapist go about helping individuals and families create healthier relationship systems? I think that the most important thing family therapists do is the same thing all good therapists to; they *listen empathically*. They are mindful; they really hear, with a nonjudgmental attitude, each individual's story. A difference with family therapy is that if the therapist is listening, other family members may listen too, perhaps with more openness and less defensiveness than usual. Sometimes people just need to be heard in order to move on. A systems oriented therapist can help families understand and explore the cultural and social contexts within which their family operates, including how such things as social class, faith, and gender beliefs effect their family system.

Here are some other things family therapists do:

- Help the family see themselves in context; see the problem behavior as part of a systemic process; learn to think systemically.
- See how the past influences the present by exploring family trees. How did a parent's experiences growing up influence their current family system? Is there a family secret? Should it be shared?
- Support, accept, normalize. Help people see that their concerns are not unique: "It's normal to feel this way when you lose your grandmother." OR "You're at the most stressful stage of the life cycle – families with young children. This is when most divorces occur. There are extreme career demands, child-rearing demands. Couples have little rest, and most don't make time for each other. What you're going through is very typical."
- Educate/teach: How to listen with empathy. How listening <u>alone</u> can help; you don't have to fix it. Also teach parenting skills; child development. Negotiation and problem-solving skills. Anger management. Communication skills like making "I" statements, and Active Listening; noting the importance of non-verbal communication. One important skill is the ability to meta-communicate, communicate about the communication. For instance, "We're having a hard time hearing each other." Or, "We're just getting more and more angry."
- It's also very useful to help people to think in terms of different people having different experiences or different points of view– instead of arguing about what is true or who is right.
- A family systems therapist might become a coach –

helping people find and practice ways of behaving in order to change a relationship or to improve the health of their family system.

Chapter 17

Summing Up

Families in the U.S. and Japan participated in a home interview in which each family member completed a true/false questionnaire describing their family. Couples, and later the family as a whole, then discussed items on which they had disagreed and tried to reach agreement. The family then completed a family picture together. The family was given colored circles for people, red and black lines of different lengths to stretch between them to show similarity or difference, and loops made of yarn to show individual boundaries, coalitions and larger groups. All of the activities were taped. Later, research team members coded the tapes for various family measures – like mood, problem-solving ability, respect, caring, and conflict.

Some twenty-five years after the home interviews, family members (both elder parents and the midlife adult former adolescents) participated in telephone interviews focusing on wellbeing and on the relationships between the adult children and their elder parents. For the U.S. sample, home interviews then followed with the now elder couples, and also with the then adult children who had families with adolescents of their own. For the adult children's families, the original interview was repeated in order for us to compare families across the generations.

The ideas of connection and individuation in the family system anchored our research. Connection involves affection and caring, creating a warm and supportive family climate that nurtures self-esteem and trust. Individuation involves respect for individuality, acknowledgement and validation of each person's ideas and feelings. Individuation in the family supports the development of a personal identity and an ability for autonomous behavior.

Healthier families had healthier adolescents. And family effects could still be seen 25 years later, when the adolescents were midlife adults. Healthier families led to greater wellbeing in the adult children, and to stronger relationships between adult children and elder parents. We also found that good relationships with the adult children supported elder parents' wellbeing. The effects of the family system experienced by adolescents could even be seen in the families created by those adolescents when they became parents. We also found that when parents set out to create some changes in their own families – to be different from the families they grew up in, they were able to enhance connection and individuation and to decrease the amount of conflict.

Marriages may get better as a married couple moves through life. My husband and I shared a very common marital dynamic: I wanted more affection; he wanted more acknowledgement and respect. Earlier in the marriage, and especially when we were raising children, we didn't have, or didn't take, the time to really address this issue as it came up. So tension would build. Once a year, on our anniversary, we would leave the children with grandparents for a few days and go off by ourselves. We would have a fight where we would each express our anger. I would be angry about his not giving me enough affection. He would be angry about my not giving him enough respect. Talking would bring us back into sync with each other, and we'd enjoy more affection and respect, less anger, deeper connection, and greater individuation. Over the years, we came to recognize our "dance" and cut it short. We would just skip to the end. And over time, we gradually got better at both connecting and individuating, expressing both love and respect.

Looking at the elder parents in our sample, we found that their marriages also improved with time. They became warmer and more supportive. Couples had more comfort with differences and less hidden conflict in elder life than they had at midlife. This could be in part because they had more couple time after the children grew up. Or, like my husband and me, over time they just got gradually better at both connection and individuation, enjoying both more love and more respect as the marriage progressed.

Family Pictures

I n case you have been wondering where the family pictures in this book came from, here are the instructions given to the families in the research project:

A FAMILY PICTURE

Use these materials to describe your family.

The circles are for people, the red and black strips are to show a relationship between two people: <u>red</u> is to show that people are <u>similar</u> in some way; <u>black</u> is to show that people are <u>different</u>. The blue yarn circles are "boundary markers." They are for showing a person who is somehow separate, or a pair or a group of people who belong together. A boundary around one person may be used to show that he or she keeps to themselves a lot, for instance, or a boundary could be used to show that two people have something special going between them--something that others in the family are not a part of.

Choose a circle for each family member. Place them on the board any way you wish. Use the red and black strips and the blue boundary markers any way that feels right to you in order to describe your family. You may choose NOT to use them at all.

You may wish to include on the board relatives or close friends of any or all of you.

The only rule is that you are not to write on the board. Work at your "picture" until it feels right. There is no right or wrong way to do this.

Do it together; we want your combined picture of your family.

In our study, pets were often included in the pictures. One family even said, "The dog came into the family to bring us together." We also found that the extremes of closeness – very close or very distant family relations – were often a sign of difficult family relationships, of less healthy functioning. As mentioned earlier, some families included a family boundary, but some did not. Most families did not include friends within a family boundary, but some did.

Making family pictures can also be helpful to people in therapeutic or educational settings. When an individual or family creates a family picture it can be a powerful tool for enhancing their understanding of the family and increase self-awareness for individuals. I have had people in therapy include deceased family members within the family boundary. This often leads to grief work around the losses.

You can be creative in making your own family picture. You can create a picture of your current family or pick a particular age, when you were a teenager, maybe – or in elementary school. Or pick a time when you remember your family being the happiest or the last time everyone was still at home. This picture is about your perceptions of your family. There is no right or wrong way to make it.

You can also make the picture with the whole family participating, or just the parents, the sibs, whatever is comfortable for you. One way to start is to draw a figure (circle, square, star; or choose a picture of an animal) to represent each family member, and anyone else who may have been part of your family, even if not biologically or legally related. You can also include pets. Place these in a way that shows who is close to whom. Then put in boundary markers, as in the instructions above – and/or choose different colored or different types of lines to show relationships between people. Anything that captures your perceptions and feelings about your family is useful.

Further Reading

The Dynamics of Connection: How Evolution and Biology Create Caregiving and Attachment by David C. Bell

Ego Development: Conceptions and Theories by Jane Loevinger

Emotion, Social Relationships, and Health by Carol D. Ryff and Burton H. Singer

The Expanding Family Life Cycle by Monica McGoldrick and Nydia A. Garcia Preto

Family Paradigms: The Practice of Theory in Family Therapy by Larry L. Constantine

Genograms: Assessment and Intervention by Monica McGoldrick and Randy Gerson

Normal Family Process by Froma Walsh

Selected Papers From The Research Project

www.familylegacies.net

Bell, L. G. (2018). A Prospective Longitudinal Study of Family from Generation to Generation, The Family Journal, 26, 411-421. [Chapter 14]

Bell, L. G. and Harsin, A. (2018). A Prospective Longitudinal Study of Marriage from Midlife to Later Life, Couple and Family Psychology: Research and Practice, 7, 12-21. [Chapter 15]

Bell, L. G. (2015). Adolescent family affects adult well-being in Japan and the U.S. Archives of Scientific Psychology, 3, 138-149. [Chapter 12]

Bell, L. D. & D. C. Bell (2012). Positive relationships that support elder health and wellbeing are grounded in midlife/adolescent family. Family and Community Health, 35, 276-286. [Chapter 13]

Bell, L. G. and Bell, D. C. (2009). Effects of family connection and family individuation. Attachment and Human Development, 11, 471-490. [Chapter 12]

Bell, L. G., Meyer, J., Rehal, D., Swope, C., Martin, D. R. and Lakhani, A. (2007). Connection and Individuation as Separate and

Independent Processes: A Qualitative Analysis. Journal of Family Psychotherapy, 18(4), 43-59. [Chapters 2, 4, 5,6,7]

Bell, L. G. and Bell, D. C. (2005). Family dynamics in adolescence affect midlife wellbeing. Journal of Family Psychology, 19, 198-207. [Chapter 12]

Bell, L. G., Dendo, H., Nakata, Y., Bell, D. C., Munakata, T., and Nakamura, S. (2004). The experience of family in Japan and the United States: Working with the constraints inherent in cross-cultural research, Journal of Comparative Family Studies, 35, 351-373. [Chapter 8]

Bell, L. G., Bell, D. C. and Nakata, Y. (2001). Triangulation and Adolescent Development in the U. S. and Japan, Family Process, 40, 173-186. [Chapter 9]

Bell, L. G and D. C. Bell. (2000). Japanese and U.S. marriage experiences: Traditional and non-traditional perceptions of family, Journal of Comparative Family Studies, 32., 309-319. [Chapter 8]

Bell, D. C., Bell, L. G., Nakata, Y. and Bell, E. M. (1996). Connection and individuality in Japan and the United States: Gender, culture, and conceptions of family health. Journal of Gender, Culture, and Health, 1, 277-294. [Chapter 8]

Bell, L. G. (1992). Song Without Words, In R. Simon, C. Barrilleaux, M. S. Wylie, and L. M. Markowitz (Eds.), The Evolving Therapist, New York: Guilford, 81 - 86. (reprinted from The Family Therapy Networker, 1989). [Chapter 8]

Bell, L. G., L. Ericksen, C. Cornwell, & D. C. Bell. (1991). Experienced closeness and distance among family members. Contemporary Family Therapy, 13, 231-245. [Chapter 2]

Nakata, Y., H. Dendo, L. Bell, N. Nakamura, S. Nakamura, I. Sasama, K. Kawanami, D. Bell, & T. Munakata. (1991). Family functioning of adolescents' families: Study of assessment of family health. Japanese Journal of Family Therapy, 8, 40-53. [Chapter 10]

Bell, L. G., C. Cornwell, & D. C. Bell. (1988) Peer relationships of adolescent daughters: A reflection of family relationship patterns, Family Relations, 37, 171-174. [Chapter 11]

Bell, L. G. (1986). Using the Family Paper Sculpture for education, therapy, and research. Contemporary Family Therapy, 8, 291-300. [Family Pictures]

Bell, L. G. & D. C. Bell. (1984). Family climate and the role of the female adolescent: Determinants of adolescent functioning. In D. H. Olson and B. C. Miller (eds.), Family Studies Yearbook, Vol. II (pp. 295-303), Beverly Hills: Sage. (Reprinted from Family Relations, 1982, 31, 519-527). [Chapter 10]